Snow Day

poems by

Evan Vandermeer

Finishing Line Press
Georgetown, Kentucky

Snow Day

ACKNOWLEDGMENTS

Eunoia Review: "Hush"
Euphemism: "The Next Generation"
Grand Little Things: "The Island"
Jersey Devil Press: "Aerophobia"
MacQueen's Quinterly: "Sleepwalking"
San Antonio Review: "Writing Haiku"
Southern Florida Poetry Journal: "Semyonovsky Square, 1849"
Twyckenham Notes: "Back to the Island," "Breakfast at the Lake House," "In the Hot
Tub"

Publisher: Leah Huete de Maines
Editor: Christen Kincaid
Cover Art: Megan Vandermeer
Author Photo: Christopher Newman
Cover Design: Elizabeth Maines McCleavy

Order online: www.finishinglinepress.com
also available on amazon.com

Author inquiries and mail orders:
Finishing Line Press
PO Box 1626
Georgetown, Kentucky 40324
USA

Contents

Climb Mt. Fuji,
O Snail,
but slowly, slowly.
                    —Issa

The Oak Tree

We've retraced our steps twice, now,
and can't seem to find Calhoun Hall, which houses
the school's Department of Economics. Whether it did
forty years ago, when he was a student here,
I don't know. Still, I'd like to see it, to imagine him
walking up the front steps with a friend
or two, some books under their arms, the sun
shining down. We have to be close—here's Benson Hall,
which according to the map is pretty much right next to it.
But we pause: spotting a QR code on Benson's sign,
she scans it with her phone, triggering a brief recorded lecture
about the building's history, and about a nearby oak tree
that predates the entire campus. Intrigued,
we forget about Calhoun and loop around the building
searching for the oak, going from tree to tree
reading their descriptive labels, which
in the failing light we have to squint to see.

The Island

As a boy, I once caught a snake in the yard
and discovered, to my horror,
their bellies open up in a slit to shit.
You wouldn't believe
how prodigiously
that small creature
filled my hands with its excrement,
which I dropped with the snake
like so much coiled Play-Doh, before running
to my father. Later, he told me about
a childhood bully
who lived down the street from him,
and how this bully enjoyed
catching garter snakes, which he'd pin down,
head and tail, with stones,
and fetching gasoline from the garage
he'd douse one, strike a match, and kick off the stones
to watch it, the snake, take off like a ribbon
furied by wind. This was something he did
on weekends, maybe, and often, so long
as he had an audience, and maybe even that
didn't matter. Meanwhile, my father avoided him,
but he once pulled a chair
out from under a classmate, who fell,
like I fell, into the sharp underbrush
on a hot summer day
so long ago, when a friend's family
brought me with them to the lake, where
we paddled out to an offshore island.
It was wild and uncultivated
but for a few short stretches of overgrown
paths, which we split up and exhausted, quickly,
and reconvening in the middle agreed that the island,
indeed, was small. But when it came time to leave
and we sat in the car, waiting
for their mom, who'd left something behind
in the steaming sand,
this friend of mine pulled down his trunks
and made his sister kiss him there. I let the phone ring,
from then on, and didn't see him again, not until

our rec league soccer teams faced off
a year later, when after the game
our teams lined up to shake hands and he chose,
instead, to punch me in the mouth, and so raised
the thunder of a father.

Writing Haiku

"It's a pleasure to name things
as long as one doesn't get
hung up about it."
    —*Jeffrey Harrison, "The Names of Things"*

I have spent much of the past year
immersing myself in haiku—taking long walks
along the ponds north of our home, a notebook
in hand; meeting monthly with a trio
of seasoned haiku poets to learn
from their vision; reading the classics
like Basho, whose poems I rehearse as I lie in bed
and fail to slip into sleep.

But in trying to write my own haiku,
I have struggled to reckon with my astonishing ignorance
of flora and fauna, the precise naming of which
is central to evoking an original experience
for the reader. Even now, I am being tested: a large black bird
struts in front of me in the slush, and in its fruitless pecking
I know there resides a poem—but I am unable to write it
because I cannot tell a raven from a crow.

Monkeys

As our little boat drifts
closer to shore,
two women next to us
giggle with anticipation
to feed the wild monkeys, whose small dark
shapes can now be seen in the treeline.
We have been traveling here long enough
to know better. When we first arrived—
before our own inevitable disillusionment—
we stopped for lunch at an open-air restaurant
on our way up to a sacred site,
and out of nowhere a woman screamed
as a tiny macaque
bounded its way across the tables
to where she sat, snatched the chapati
right from her hand, and swung back out the way he came
using the roof's low-hanging rafters, mocking
our name for such things on the playground.
Less than a week later, we were left
in the Rajasthani heat an entire afternoon
because of a fat, long-fanged monkey
stationed at the top of the stairs
leading to our hostel's entrance, where he hissed
and flexed at those who tried to approach.
Looking down at the scene
from a window, the hostel's proprietor shrugged
and gave us a look that asked,
What can be done? And yet,
this didn't keep us from visiting
the so-called Monkey Temple, though
we were on our guard
as we passed through its crumbling gates.
The whole ruined outdoor complex—
as if for an Indiana Jones movie set—was utterly silent
and seemingly deserted. Not until a tourist
coming in behind us
pulled out some peanuts
did the numberless tribe

emerge from their shadowed combs,
with one (the leader?) even riding a pig
like a warhorse. We froze, and watched
as a lowly monkey grunt
made its cautious way
up to the man with the peanuts, and after
feinting for the one held out to it
in the man's right hand
it struck, sudden as lightning, for the whole bag
held back in his left, which it grabbed
like the woman's chapati
and raced back to its spot in line, victorious…
But who would believe such things, I think,
especially that bit with the pig? Not even
someone who already hates monkeys, like me,
would buy such a ridiculous tale, let alone
those already seduced by monkeys' alluring
resemblance to our kind. But I have to try
to warn them—each with a purse
bulging with belongings, I know
the trouble that spells.

In Rishikesh

An author I admire wrote, once, about a trip to India
where he lost his religious yearnings. In college,
he considered becoming a monk, having found inspiration in Merton's
Seven Story Mountain. But when he got to Calcutta and began volunteering
in a sick house, he befriended a rather crude stranger
whose company, finally, he preferred
to the soft-spoken palliative care volunteers, and that was that.

Five years ago, on my own trip to India, we went to Rishikesh
and got into a tuk-tuk accident. It was night, we had just arrived by train,
and a man on a moped slammed into our side while trying to pass us
as we turned. We were fine, but he flew over the hood
and left a trail of brain on the street behind him. Within minutes
a crowd had formed around the body, and someone, after fishing
the phone from the man's pocket, called who turned out to be

the brother, who arrived in minutes on his own moped
and knelt beside the body. To our amazement, the man then sat up
like the resurrected dead, and shaking his head as if waking
from a nap, he looked around in panic for the bag of lentil soup
that had sat on his lap as he tried to speed around us,
the same soup now streaked along the moonlit street. Disappointed,
he hopped on his brother's moped and rode off into the night.

I'd Tell You

How walking onto set of a Bollywood film
as aspiring extras—our hostel's owner
having made a few calls to give us a shot—
we were shocked to be pointed at, immediately,
by an important-looking man with a clipboard

from across the warehouse, a man who,
clearly unsatisfied by the hundreds of options
swarming before him, must have had a vision
the moment he saw us, for he parted the crowd
like a Biblical sea, summoned us over

to size us up, and nodded slowly, with gravitas,
making a sign to some clipboardless man
to fetch us the clothes we'd wear for our roles:
four Western-looking bartenders, legitimized
by dazzling black vests that didn't quite fit.

Dressed in new garb, we were led to a roped-off
area in the back, where with the other extras
we marveled at our good fortune, and mingled
with a tall, gorgeous Polish woman whose dream
was to make it as a Bollywood star, her obsession

since childhood. We were mesmerized by her
dusky beauty, by her totally bizarre path to acting,
which she was in the middle of describing
when, at the sound of a whistle, we four bartenders
were whisked into place behind a marble counter,

where we stood for the following thirteen hours
and pretended to fix drinks, and, between takes,
practiced twirling cocktail shakers in our open palms
with the gravity-defying flair only bartenders
who love being bartenders know how to pull off.

For what felt like ages, the focus of the scene
was so far across set that we couldn't make it out,
but some kind of procession was clearly
heading our way, and by the time it arrived we'd
each mastered the mixer spin, and confidently spun

as the cameras rolled, even when faced by Aishwarya
Rai, former Miss Universe, one of the leads, who sat
three feet down the bar at the center of the world,
it seemed, and whose eye between scenes I finally caught
and performed the new trick I'd so expertly learned...

Two months later, by sheer luck, the movie was released
while we were still in the country, so we went to see it
on opening night. By that time, we had talked
so much about it, with such burning anticipation,
that it didn't even feel real. But of course, they cut the scene.

Flotsam

What began as a casual audit
of the hundreds of used books
boxed away in my mother's garage
has become an unpromising quest
for a certain photograph
of my father, which I framed
and brought with me abroad
but have somehow misplaced
since returning. In the photo,
he is flanked on either side
by me and my twin sister,
the two of us dressed in neon blue
graduation gowns, each with golden stoles
draped around our necks. I don't recall
a single detail about that day—
not for a million dollars could I tell you
who the valedictorian was, let alone
what his or her speech was about,
or for how long it probably dragged on—
but thanks to that picture
(even if it never resurfaces),
I will never forget he was there,
sweating through his shirt...
So I keep searching for it, but before long—
with all of my teenage belongings
sprawled out around the garage
like the wreckage of a ship—I have to admit
the photo isn't here, and I return
to flipping through books, separating them
into donations and keepers, with one pile
slowly dwarfing the other.

Back to the Island

Iguanas are languid things. These,
baking in the palm-filtered sun, lie still
as fallen statues in the sand, except for the occasional
swish of muscled tail. They lie there, a parched green,
and one might think they wait. Some, nearby,
surround the boulder she claimed as hers
the last visit, when she came, alone, on her first trip abroad
since Dad died, an early morning heart attack
having brought him to the floor, right after shoveling
in a blizzard. He woke early, and must have
lain there for hours—a little blood
trickling from his head where he clipped the counter on the way down—
before my sister found him. I was off at college,
and for a while, at least, their ruse to get me home
before telling me
worked—but Mom's voice broke
on the phone, and she had to tell me then.
It felt embarrassing, or indecent, somehow, to be
in the company of others, so I went
into that same blizzard, down the road
to the wide walking path
buried in snowfall, which despite the wind
was more silent even
than the swish of a tail in sand, half a world away,
where I sit now, listening in vain. Last night,
with the sun inexorably setting over the sea,
we took a canoe
and made our way out to an island
not far from shore, an island so tame, it seemed,
we could walk its circumference. We never made it,
though—Mom stopped paddling
a dozen yards off and, closing her eyes
and breathing deeply,
made me promise to tell her of this, later,
if when on her deathbed she needs reminding
of what happened here,
of worn but brilliant skies. Once,
when I couldn't sleep, and she assured me
God always wins, I asked where God was
when the towers fell, and with all her AA wisdom she had nothing to say.

I don't blame her, but I can see
where this fear comes from, and why she drew crosses in chalk
on the window, as a girl, before bed. Where are we now,
on this side of things? And who am I
to speak of the blood, when I wasn't there to witness it?
Anyway, I promise to try.

Semyonovsky Square, 1849

"His uncertainty and his repulsion before the unknown,
which was going to overtake him immediately, was terrible."
—*The Idiot*

Long before he penned some of the greatest novels
ever written, Dostoevsky stood before a firing squad
condemned to death. He and the other revolutionaries
had been kept in dank dark cells for the previous
eight months, and were finally brought to Semyonovsky Square
in a hazy winter light that was, to their maladjusted eyes,
overwhelming. None of them seemed to believe it was possible
they'd be killed, but then they saw a peasant cart full
of what looked like coffins, and their hope for penal servitude
faltered, and promptly disappeared at the reading of their sentence,
which the tsar ordered was to hang in the air to ensure
the next and apparently last minute of their lives would be torture.
It was, and though they each denied the priest's call to confession,
none refused to kiss the cross when he held it to their cracking lips.

The Draft

The anticipation was unbearable, waiting for him to come home
on draft night, when he and the other coaches met up at the park district
and took turns selecting kids for their teams, most of them also dads
with lists of their kid's friends' names as guidance for whom to pick. Once,
he almost managed to get all eight of us—I can see him, thrilled at the draft
to have snagged seven with only one more to go, brewing up argument
for a final trade that would complete the dream team and send him home a hero,
thinking already of the impromptu practices he'd hold up the street, since

we all lived in the same neighborhood anyway—but for some reason this other guy
wouldn't budge on a trade, even though he had no idea who my friend was,
even though we were ten years old and the whole formal drafting thing was over-
serious and deeply silly. We were pretty good that year, but what I remember most
was how, when we eventually squared off against that guy's team, Dad got so
    riled up
at calls that went their way our assistant coach had to hold him back by the belt
    loop.

Aerophobia

I promised myself
that when this plane lands
I will have something
to show for it, and given
these first rumblings
of high-altitude turbulence—
the seatbelt light
having just lit up like a Christmas tree—
I better hurry
and get something presentable down
before it's too late. At least
I can lose myself (thank you,
little pink pill) in the movie
playing on the back of the headrest
directly in front of me. Without headphones,
it's a largely silent film, largely because
I've seen it enough
to hear the music and dialogue
in the back of my mind. And now,
the flight attendant wheels up
and offers an array of non-perishable snacks:
pretzels, wafers, or cookies, and like a fool
I choose the pretzels (a sad
last meal), but my wife is kind enough
to offer me one of her cookies, which
I eat so quickly in a single bite
she can't help but comment
on my inability to savor anything
but coffee, the only thing
I'll slow down to enjoy. Right then—
as if on cue—Will Ferrell's character
takes his own first sip of that black nectar
and grimaces in pain, almost as if
he had swallowed a thumbtack.

Snow Day

I had already splashed cold water
on my face, fed our eager pets, brushed
the morning breath from my mouth, and sat
on a cushion for thirty minutes, counting to ten
while staring at a wall, when I heard
the good news: work, school, the whole town, basically,
gets a snow day, given that *blowing and drifting snow*
could bring a potentially lethal travel situation
with wind chills falling below zero. I'm too awake
to go back to bed, too stimulated by rejoicing endorphins,
so I whisper *snow day* to my sleeping wife,
turn off her alarm—knowing she'll sleep
for another couple hours, now—and begin to brew
some coffee, which I plan to enjoy while reading a book.
But then, to my surprise, she trots out of our room
with a light in her eyes, just as thrilled and unable to sleep
as I am, doing a little dance
on the living room rug—and it occurs to me
that until we're retired, this could very well be
the last true snow day we ever have, where
with hardly any responsibilities
we can just sit and do nothing, nothing but watch
the snow coming down to cover the earth
in a silencing blanket of white.

In the Hot Tub

Perhaps the best part about skiing
is finishing skiing, grabbing robes
from the hotel closet, and taking glasses of Grand Marnier
out to the hot tub, where we sit
long beyond the recommended limit
as the booze rushes to our heads
and we make ourselves bubble beards,
giddy with contentment. But you stayed
in today, so it's just me and your father out here,
pruning in silence. Before long, though,
we've drunk enough to loosen up—
two quiet men, he nearly half a century older—
and soon he grows garrulous, telling me
about his tenth and fiftieth reunions,
how after all that time
his old Milwaukee neighborhood
was completely unchanged, except
for the size of the trees. He tells me, too,
about seeing his best man
for the first time in many, many years,
but when I ask if the reunion
helped them reconnect, he doesn't quite
say yes. Our drinks finished,
I see that his large sagging eyes—
a misty cataract blue, but naturally so—
are glassy, and they shine through the steam
he's wreathed in, which rises from his body,
I can't help but think, like the past burning off.

Eight Weeks Five Days

Three times this month, now, we've been called in
for a surprise ultrasound. Each visit has been the same—
the silence of the waiting room, the silence
of the world outside, the wind tossing
the darkening leaves, all seen through clear stained-glass
windows, their silver flowers frozen. And now, the technician's silence
as she probes my wife; and our own, which descends
like a sheet shaken out, maybe, and falling
in some windless place.

Roosevelt

While using a pitcher to refill the water bowl
of our English spot, he tries to drink from the stream
as if it were a stream, and I have to brush him aside
with the back of my hand, using the force it would take
to part a curtain of silk.

As soon as I'm finished, he returns to the bowl
and dips his small, whiskered face in the water just so, sipping
with faint little squeaks befitting his fragility. When he's done,
he hops to his spot at the front of the room, uses his paws to pull
down his ears, and cleans them.

His name is Roosevelt, a name he was given
by the widowed hoarder he was rescued from, a woman
who christened all the poor caged animals in her basement
after American presidents, whom now that I think about it
she either loved or hated.

Sleepwalking

Twice this week upon waking,
I've found the bed frame
a good six inches from where it was
the night before.

There's a black streak on the wall
marking its mysterious, scraping course.
I have no memory of movement to explain this,
but I suppose it's possible

there's violence to my tossing. If not violence, then
something else—maybe fear. My room in Prague
was small, trapezoidal, with one wall
that slanted from floor to ceiling,

a wall she watched me struggle against,
like Atlas, asleep but feverish and straining
under the weight, a heroic somnambulator
whose gift was unconsciousness

—an echo, perhaps, of wading out
into the moonlit lake
and being found, waist-deep in the glossy stillness,
still dreaming.

The Next Generation
For Samuel

I met your father our freshman year of college,
when the whole English department
gathered for general remarks
to kick off the fall semester. I took the open seat
next to him, and after some small talk
cut right to the chase, asking
if he ever played basketball,
my surest litmus test for friendship
at the time. He said that he did,
and I resolved, then, that he would be
my first college friend. Not long after, we made plans
to play at the campus rec center,
and when we did, I had the distinct privilege
to witness an absolute shitshow, your father
about as out of place on the freethrow line
as a riled-up horse in a jewelry shop.
Confused by his unfamiliarity with the game
and basic lack of athleticism—so evident
in his movements on the court, in his
handling of the ball—I wondered aloud
why he told me he played. *Well*, he explained,
I don't really play, but technically I've played.
In the years since, he has demonstrated
a distressingly profound clumsiness
countless times—breaking more glasses
than I now own, shattering light fixtures at restaurants
when lifting his arms in greeting, and even
spilling all the breast milk on the night
they brought you home, reducing your mother
to tears. Even tonight, at your first-ever Christmas party
with the whole gang, he brought his elbow down
on the back of my chair, yelled out in pain, and dropped some dice
on the hardwood floor, which carried them away
as he toppled a pile of cards with his bear-like hand, a hand
transformed, somehow, when later that night
it cupped your head on the living room rug
and he showed me, with patience, how to change you.

Breakfast at the Lake House

It's not that we're terminally ill,
or that we have some morbid death wish,
but when our friends begin to discuss
their investment portfolios, two of us
grow quiet, focusing instead on breakfast,
which we have been tasked with cooking
this morning. It's a foreign concept to those who,
like us, struggle to believe we'll live long enough
to cash in on the returns. Maybe it's just
a failure of imagination, though
I once shared this half-joking
half-belief with a therapist, and he said
it's not uncommon for sons
who've lost their fathers in youth
to believe that they, too, are destined
to get swept away before their time
has come. That would account for me—
note the faint and infernal rash on my chest,
a blooming, surely, of some underlying condition—
but not for my friend, my co-chef, for whom
a long line of SSRIs have failed in their duty
pretty much absolutely. And so, standing at the stove
while conversation unfolds, we narrow our attention
on the labor at hand, me stirring eggs into golden shapes
while he tends to hash browns he shredded himself,
checking their undersides now and again
to mark the level of burn.

Hush

He loved Bruce Springsteen, whose Greatest Hits
was one of the few cassettes he kept
in the center console of his Jeep Wrangler.
He'd hush the whole family
when certain songs were up,
and as he sang along
he'd drum his index finger on the wheel,
which until the very end was sheathed
in the fake leather cover I got him for Christmas
as a boy, when they handed out cash
and set us kids loose in the dollar store.
He was old enough then to have former lives,
and to know that music could return him to them,
which is probably why he'd hush us
when "Thunder Road" opened with its bright,
plaintive harmonica: to slip back
into that version of himself
that hadn't yet sacrificed his 20s
on alcohol's altar, leading a loser life in his parents'
basement doing nothing but drinking
and training for triathlons. But then he got sober,
and after meeting a woman at AA
eloped with her, eventually throwing
his hands in the air
as if he had finished an Ironman race
when she whispered *twins*.
What brought them together
explains why the fridge
had nothing but LaCroix,
which they'd bring in a cooler
to the neighborhood block parties
they rarely attended, the other adults
not quite getting it. Still, there was compensation:
at one such party in the Hoods' front yard,
they made a scene wrestling in the grass
for control of the garden hose, playing
with water—their drink, at least until
we were teens. That one summer, we spent a weekend
at Tybee Island, and he got so stunningly blasted each night

he'd pass out on the beach, where
we had no choice but to leave him as the surf threatened to rake him in.
He admitted, after, that he was powerless
and ill, and stopped just in time,
for Mom had the bags packed and the car running.
I think of her, now, on those hot summer nights
as he sat out back, alone,
gulping down beer and staring
into the fire pit, the flames' shadows curling around him
while she stayed inside watching reruns of *Grey's Anatomy*.
Perhaps she remembered those nights
in the dry years that followed,
when he cranked down the window
and started to drum
with the hands I inherited,
and perhaps that's why she'd hush us, too,
and let the man sing.

Evan Vandermeer was born and raised in north Chicagoland. He received a BA in English from Illinois State University, and an MA in English with a concentration in creative writing from Indiana University South Bend. He won a Touchstone Award for his haibun "The Shape of a Life" in 2024, and his other poems have appeared in *San Antonio Review, Southern Florida Poetry Journal, Twyckenham Notes*, and elsewhere. He was recently featured in A New Resonance 14, and his haiku and haibun have also appeared in *Acorn, contemporary haibun online, Frogpond, Kingfisher, Modern Haiku*, and other journals that specialize in Japanese short forms. He lives outside Nashville, Tennessee, with his wife and two daughters. Snow Day is his first poetry collection.